PREFACE

Hi. Some of my cartoons in this book are R-rated. I included them because they're funny. Hopefully the reader will agree and will enjoy my wicked sense of humor.

— SJV

My Wicked World of
Gag Cartoons

SPECIAL EDITION

ISBN: 978-0-9620303-6-9

LCCN: 2021903165

Published by Volkano Books

Miami, Florida USA

Introduction

As a kid growing up in mid 20th century America, the classic gag cartoons that appeared weekly in The Saturday Evening Post and The New Yorker were my inspiration and teachers.

In the spirit of paying a debt forward, I hope my cartoons in this book will inspire new cartoonists to see their next blank sheet as the matrix of a future masterpiece that will make the world smile.

Josh

S. J. VOLK

"Some snoopy kid discovered
Miss Liberty is a Mister."

"Have mercy, Lord!... Mrs. Noah's dress has already shrunk 2 inches above her ankles!"

"On the brighter side, if we'll give our space secrets to the terrorists, they'll be able to blast off to another planet, and good riddance*!*"

"He exhausted himself chasing me around his penthouse, so by the end of the evening, I was still chaste*!*"

“Hey**…** we came here to plant a **FLAG***!*”

"Damn*!* I warned you not to tell anyone. Now everybody wants to abduct an Earthling*!*"

“Yes, but what have you written **LATELY**?”

"Oh..Oh.. Looks like we're in for a whirlwind courtship!"

"It's a great concept, but I predict the series won't survive even the first season."

" If education is compulsory, how come I'm still ignorant? "

"Sir, now that your bronchitis is cured, how about coughing up your bill?"

"I offered to give their leaders the solutions to war, poverty, and disease...but the only thing they wanted to talk about was Flying Saucers!"

"Would anybody in this theater of war
like to go to the powder room?"

ACME
CLEANING
and
PRESSING
ACME
THE CUSTOMER
IS ALWAYS
RIGHT!
BUT DON'T PRESS
YOUR LUCK.

" I'm going to be awarded some kind of peace prize. Thanks to my book, it's the first time in history that all nations were united in condemning an author's work*!* "

“What’s the SCORE, dad ?”

"You should be a magazine publisher.
You make an issue out of everything*!*"

MARRIAGE
COUNCELLING
JOSH

"And if elected, I promise an annual **tithe** refund."

"I think the purple pill is working on the wrong end."

"No..No..General, you don't declare peace ON another country!"

"If success is 1% talent and 99% sweat, maybe I should move to a warmer climate."

"Don't be a fool, prince. It's better to be than not to be!"

"It may be a giant leap for mankind, but from up here, it looks like just another depressed area."

“If you ask me, it’s just a **MYTH!**”

"At last they're performing my plays in plain English! Finally I'll be able to understand what I've written!"

“Most people don’t realize the REAL tragedy is that my book isn’t selling*!*”

"At that price, it should be called a ***dollarly***, not a quarterly*!*"

NUDIST COLONY
CLOSED
LEAP FROG GAMES WILL BE CONTINUED IN HOSPITAL GYMNASIUM.

"C'mon down, Mr. Finley, don't be a sissy*!*"

ACME
DRUG
CO.
RAGWEED

UNITED
NATIONS
NO LANGUAGE GAP
JOSH

"All in favor of solving the problem by turning the sales chart a quarter turn to the left!"

"Say AAA"

"At first I agreed to do it because I thought ORAL meant to just TALK."

"Nag..Nag..Nag! If Moses had been married to you, he would've stayed on the mountain*!*"

"Doc, do you think it's a sign of effeminacy?
I'm beginning to understand my wife."

"If you're right, and we really are immortal spirits whose purpose on Earth is to generate love, then you need to just shut the f—k up and kiss me."

"Don't tell the boys in Accounting, but I still count numbers all day**...** force of habit."

"My book got mixed reviews today. I tripped and my manuscript blew all over town!"

FR
EMB
CH
SY

"Mrs. Fleegle, if you think I'M guilty, there's really no point in my taking your case."

NO J-WALKING

NO J-WALKING

~~NO~~ J-WALKING
II

"I'll bet it's smart enough to clean itself, but it doesn't want to cause a labor problem."

"O.K. Officer, write the damn ticket... but don't expect me to save your ass on Judgment Day."

"Don't laugh, stupid.
We're all in the same boat!"

"It's the Latin name for the tree."

RESTAURANT
RED HOT
CHICKEN
TO
TAKE OUT
LOSH

"Let's not knock the crackpot fringe. Compared to their fantastic stories, our accounts are almost believable."

"Wow! these modern trains sure can travel."

" **Exorcise** always gives me an appetite."

"And then I was assigned to do a 2-week undercover story on the homeless, but I don't remember anything after that."

"I've cancelled my vacation. I'm afraid the faculty will discover the school can run better without me."

"Mom, if it means to make love, why is f—k a dirty word?"

"I'm the interior decorator."

"You can air my story now as science fiction, or next year as a factual historical documentary."

CYTIBANK

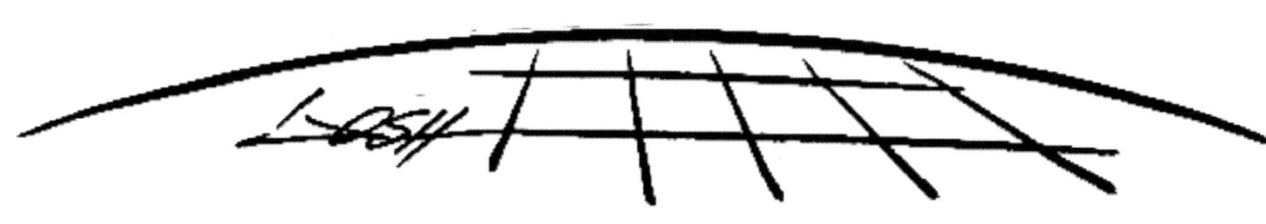

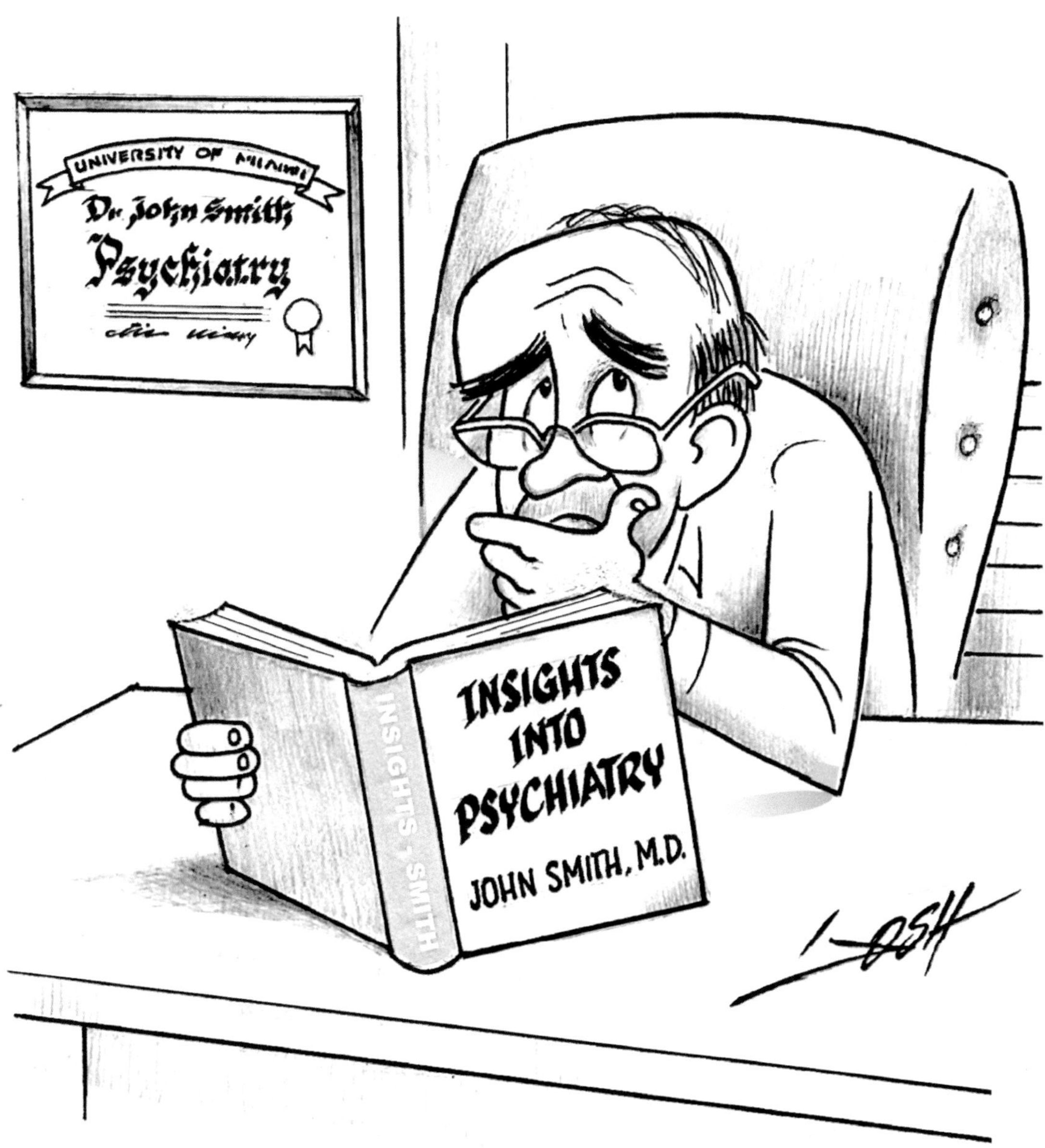

"Hmm… I wonder what I meant by **THAT.**"

USED CARS
GROCE
LEMONS
LOSH

"One more strike and we're out."

BUY
CHICKEN
SOUP

"I call it **FREEDOM.**"

"It's all my PHALT!"

"Sorry you misunderstood.
We sell only **non-herbal** tea."

"I can do a little of everything*!*"

“My husband doesn’t trust me either,
— especially with blueberry pie.”

"Will this spray get rid of 2-legged pests?"

"It must be one of those UFOs they're always writing about."

"Congratulations, Nelson! That was the fastest mile on record!"

"Sure, it was a good movie, but not as GOOD as the BOOK!"

“Shut up! I’ve got my own problems!”

"They say our marriage is shaky,
— like that's a BAD thing."

"O.K...O.K... I'll void it! But a real man would appreciate a well-trimmed hair in his wine!"

"If you ask me, the whole UFO scare is just subliminal advertising by a cigar company."

"I don't care what your grammar book says*!*
The **U.N.** is **not** just a **negative prefix***!*"

RICE FLAKES
FREE TOY INSIDE

THE
FIRE
BUG
MYSTERY

"I need your expert opinion. I'm compiling a thesaurus of obscene words."

"O.K. O.K. I'll be your agent*!*"

"Until the next office party, Mr. Smith,
Goodnight... and good luck*!*"

“Is a proposal of marriage made in the rear seat of a journalist’s foreign car binding?”

CHILD
PSYCHOL
JOSH

"Relax*!* People say there's safety in numbers."

"The first man who designs an automatic designing machine will get $100,000 ...as severance pay."

"I just wrote a short-short on shortening and I'd like some bread in advance."

"Cheer up, Trudy...we're not alone.
I'm sure there's life on other plants."

"Nobody pushes **ME** around*!*"

"Run for your life! The Gourmet Chef is in town!"

"Stop! If you still have the strength to complain, your injuries are frivolous!"

"Would you believe she called this a **STRUMPET.**"

“Why doesn’t anybody ever believe I’m sincere?”

"If I cooked the same dinner every day, my company would go belly up too."

JOE'S
AUTO
REPAIR

"Life is a safari. If you focus on the fleas, you lose the big game."

"Why do you always have to bring your office work home with you?"

"Gentlemen, let's stop blaming each other for your failure!"

"It's a miracle they get any work done,
hanging around a joint all day."

EGO
PRESS

"This is the road to WHERE**?**"

"I don't care what kind of magic you use, just finish the job!"

"This advanced model can repair itself, but only when it's in tip-top condition."

"I notice the less time we spend making love, the more times you like to use the F-word."

"Doctor, you said I should be glad I'm left with partial feeling after the surgery. So you should be glad I'm leaving you with partial payment."

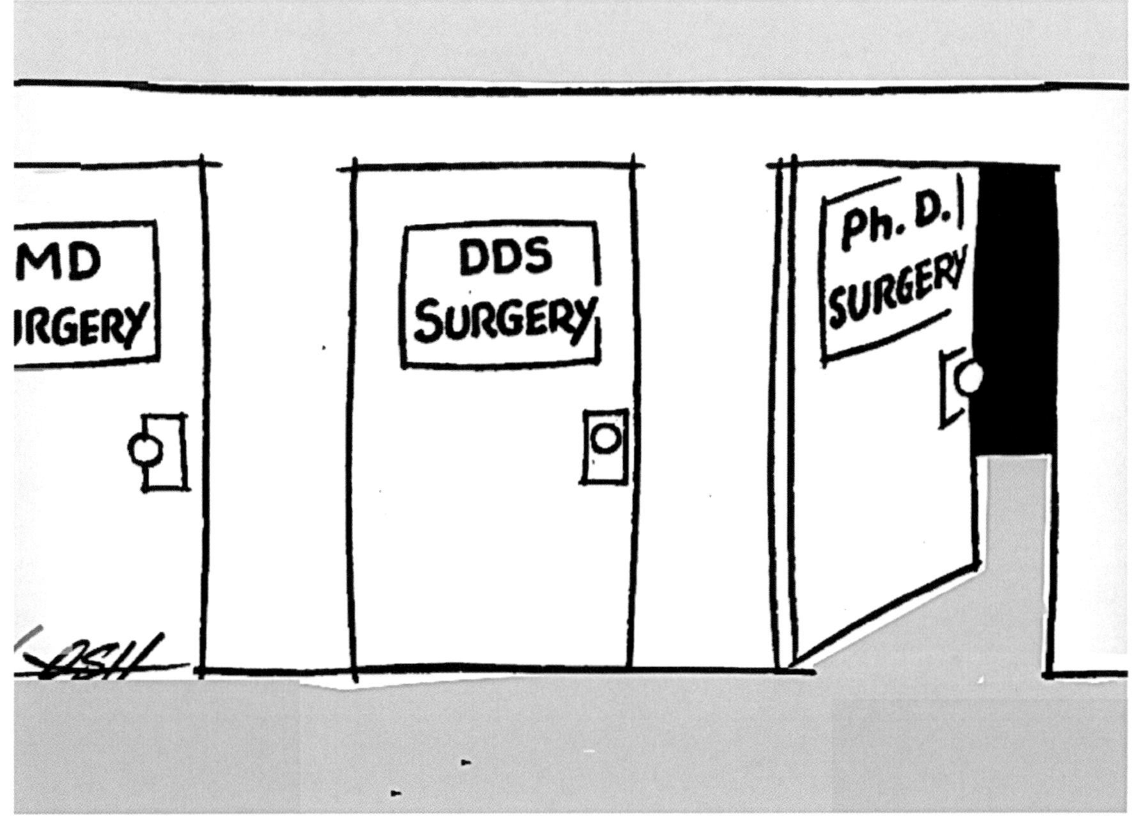

"Don't worry, Miss Nemeroff, we won't cut out all of your interior monologue."

"Sorry you misunderstood.
We interview GUEST writers."

“I threatened to kill myself if they rejected my manuscript, so they recommended a medium to contact if ever I’d get a hot idea down there.”

" Sir, I see your duplicator is in fine shape."

ASYLUM
DRIVE CAREFULLY
INMATES ESCAPING

"Oops! We still have a **FALLOUT** problem!"

“Our crazy neighbor says this will someday be called Jurassic Park in 3-D and surround sound.”

"Sir, I think you'll happily sign this county petition against door-to-door soliciting."

“This democracy system is great. I hear you’re already collecting unemployment.”

"Oh...Oh... Here comes trouble!"

"Sir, I know 21st century medicine has prolonged your lifespan, but you can't just hang around town like a vagrant."

"OOPS*!* I meant to say, '*That's one small step for **a man**, one giant leap for mankind.*' Do you think anyone noticed I forgot the '**a**' ?"

HOOKERS ARE
BUY-SEXUAL

JOSH

"It says, we forgot to say ***PLEASE.***"

"Short Anglo-Saxon words have been anathema to Fred ever since a critic called his book **CRAP.**"

"I don't know anything about city planning, but I know a decaying **molar** when I see one."

"Dad, can I borrow the UFO tonight?"

"I could've made an "A" in math too, but I ran out of ink."

" Wow*!* Thanks, Miss Twombly*!* It looks like your teaching skill is improving*!*"

"I see seven of your books will become bestsellers. You'll get huge royalties from your paperbacks and ebooks and magazine serials. Hollywood, Broadway, television, and internet giants will offer you fabulous wealth for the rights to your stories. Your inspiring song lyrics will become classics. Your newspaper column will be internationally syndicated and quoted in awe by future historians. Your incisive wit and wisdom will enlighten a myriad generations. Your philosophical insights will become required reading in universities. Your work will be translated into the languages of all inhabited planets. And this'll be ten dollars per word."

Made in the USA
Monee, IL
02 November 2021

3d797749-2731-4531-b434-534678cb762bR01